P9-DEZ-183

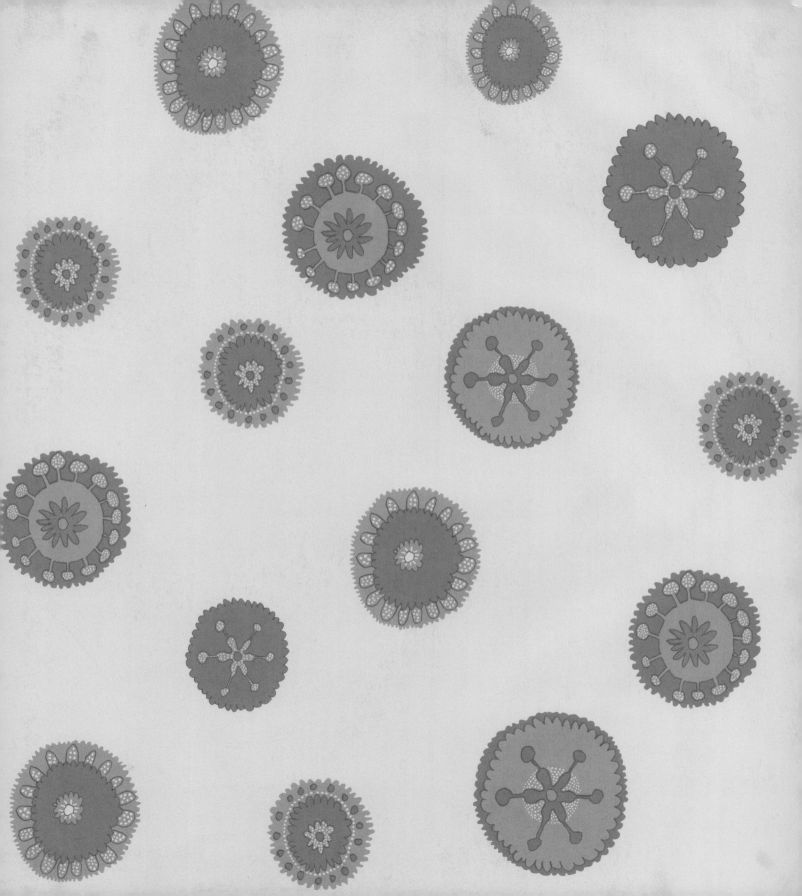

For Cooper Jacobson Reinfeld F. M.

Welcome to the world, Angelo Graves L. T.

First paperback edition 2018

Library of Congress Catalog Card Number 2014951411
ISBN 978-0-7636-7002-3 (hardcover)
ISBN 978-0-7636-9972-7 (paperback)

CCP 22 21 20 19 18 17
10 9 8 7 6 5 4 3 2 1

Printed in Shenzhen, Guangdong, China

This book was typeset in Garamouche.
The illustrations were done in ink and pencil
and assembled digitally.

Candlewick Press
99 Dover Street
Somerville, Massachusetts 02144

visit us at www.candlewick.com

Happy in Our Skin

Fran Manushkin   illustrated by Lauren Tobia

CANDLEWICK PRESS

Look at you!

You look so cute
in your brand-new birthday suit.
This is how we all begin:
small and happy in our skin.

Bouquets of babies
sweet to hold:
cocoa brown,
cinnamon,
and honey gold.

Ginger-colored babies,
peaches and cream, too—
splendid skin for me,
splendid skin for you!

It's terrific to have skin.
It keeps the outsides out
and your insides in.

As you keep growing,
your skin grows, too.
Clever skin for me,
clever skin for you.

Whoops!
When you fall,
your skin will heal
with a scab,
a perfect seal.

Sometimes
skin has freckles
or birthmarks
or dimples.

We get a tan when it's sunny,
and when it's freezing—
goose pimples!

It's delightful
to hug
and tickle
and wrestle,

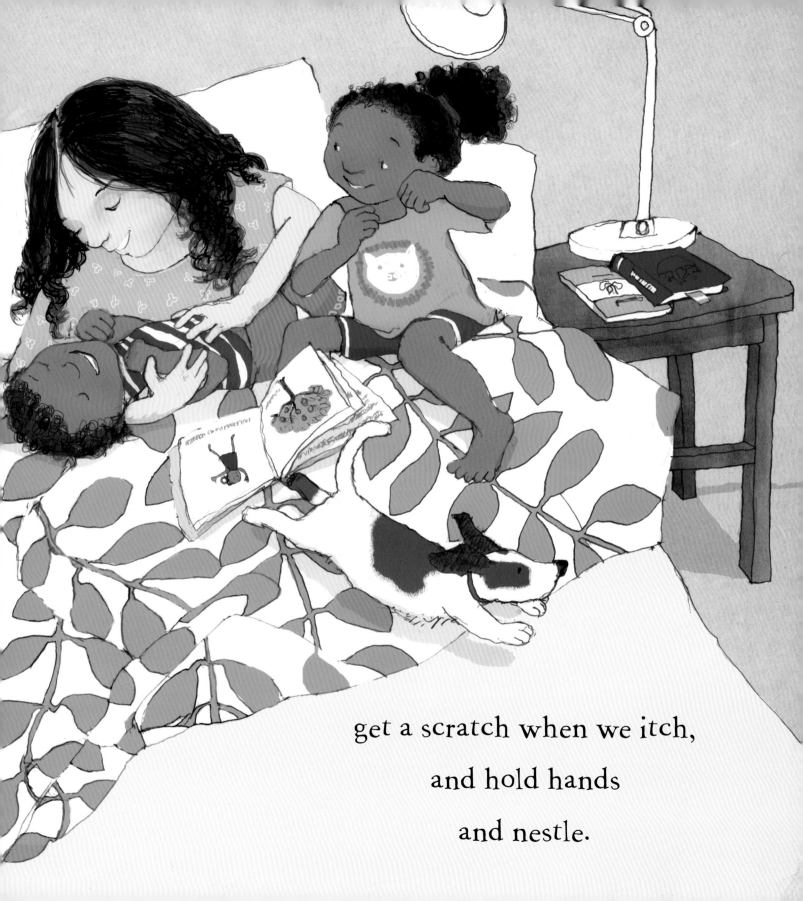

get a scratch when we itch,

and hold hands

and nestle.

Skin covers us from
head to toes.

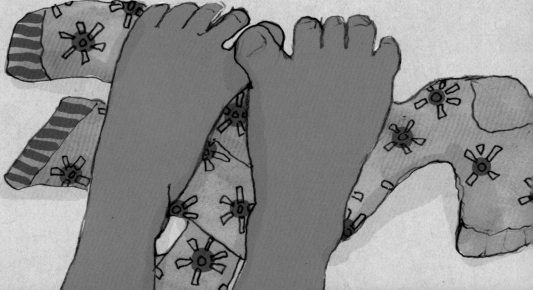

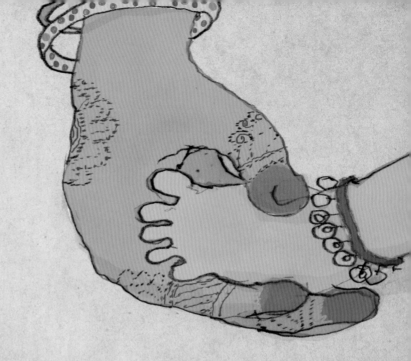

It's always there
beneath our clothes.

Yes, we all have skin,
but nobody is you.
You are one of a kind
and your fingerprints, too.

What a wonderful world!

Such a hullabaloo —

with all of us in it!

See the splendid view:

BLOCK PARTY

bouquets of people,

blooming and boisterous,

brawny and thin,

loving each day . . .

happy in our skin!

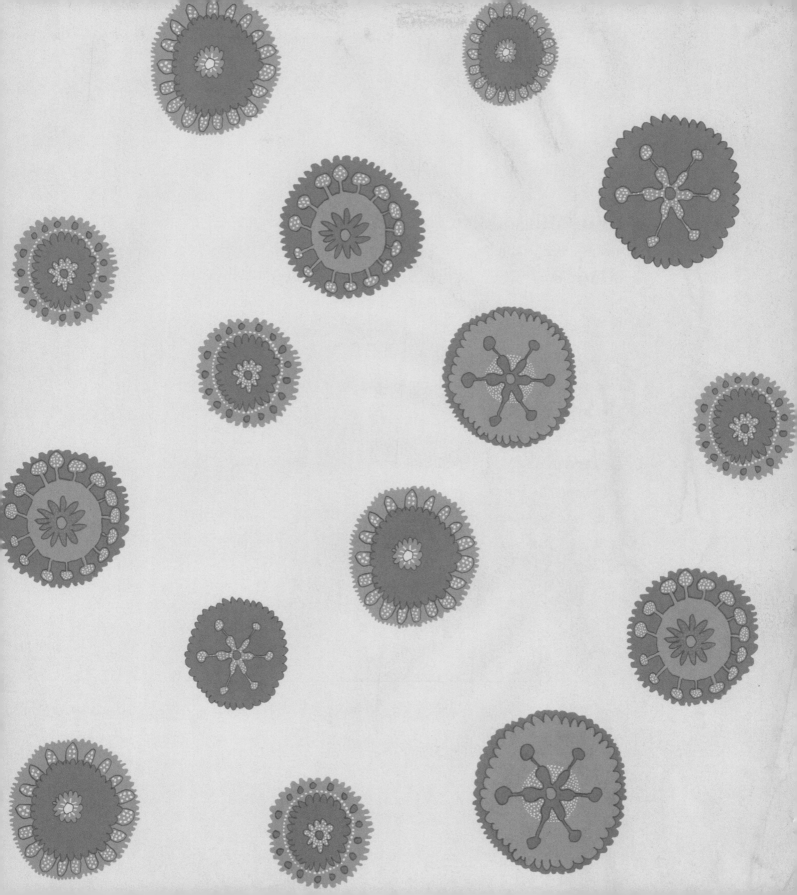

Fran Manushkin is the author of more than seventy-five books for children, including the Katie Woo series and the Pedro series, both illustrated by Tammie Lyon; *Big Girl Panties*, illustrated by Valeria Petrone; *Big Sisters Are the Best*, illustrated by Kirsten Richards; *The Tushy Book*, illustrated by Tracy Dockray; *Bamboo for Me, Bamboo for You!*, illustrated by Purificación Hernández; and *Baby, Come Out!*, illustrated by Ronald Himler and translated into eight languages. She lives in New York City.

Lauren Tobia is the illustrator of several books for children, including the Anna Hibiscus books by Atinuke; *Baby's Got the Blues* by Carol Diggory Shields; and *Are You Sure, Mother Bear?* by Amy Hest. She lives in a tiny house in Bristol, England.

12/18